LEVEL ONE (ELEMENTARY)

Trombone Student

*by Fred Weber
in collaboration with
Paul Tanner*

To The Student

This book, with the aid of a good teacher, is designed to help you become an excellent player on your instrument in a most enjoyable manner. It will take a reasonable amount of work and CAREFUL practice on your part. If you do this, learning to play should be a valuable and pleasant experience.

To The Teacher

The Belwin "Student Instrumental Course" is the first and only complete course for private instruction of all band instruments. Like instruments may be taught in classes. Cornets, trombones, baritones and basses may be taught together. The course is designed to give the student a sound musical background and at the same time provide for the highest degree of interest and motivation. The entire course is correlated to the band oriented sequence.

To make the course both authoritative and practical, most books are co-authored by a national authority on each instrument in collaboration with Fred Weber, perhaps the most widely-known and accepted authority at the student level.

The Belwin "Student Instrumental Course" has three levels: elementary, intermediate, and advanced intermediate. Each level consists of a method and three correlating supplementary books. In addition, a duet book is available for Flute, B♭ Clarinet, E♭ Alto Sax, B♭ Cornet and Trombone. The chart below shows the correlating books available with each part.

The Belwin "STUDENT INSTRUMENTAL COURSE" - A course for individual and class instruction of LIKE instruments, at three levels, for all band instruments.

EACH BOOK IS COMPLETE IN ITSELF BUT ALL BOOKS ARE CORRELATED WITH EACH OTHER

METHOD
"The Trombone Student"
For individual or Brass class instruction.

ALTHOUGH EACH BOOK CAN BE USED SEPARATELY, IDEALLY, ALL SUPPLEMENTARY BOOKS SHOULD BE USED AS COMPANION BOOKS WITH THE METHOD

STUDIES AND MELODIOUS ETUDES
Supplementary scales, warm-up and technical drills, musicianship studies and melody-like studies.

TUNES FOR TECHNIC
Technical type melodies, variations, and "famous passages" from musical literature --- for the development of technical dexterity.

THE TROMBONE SOLOIST
Interesting and playable graded easy solo arrangements of famous and well-liked melodies. Also contains 2 Duets, and 1 Trio. Easy piano accompaniments.

DUETS FOR STUDENTS
Easy duet arrangements of familiar melodies for early ensemble experience.
Available for: Flute
B♭ Clarinet
Alto Sax
B♭ Cornet
Trombone

CHART OF TROMBONE POSITIONS

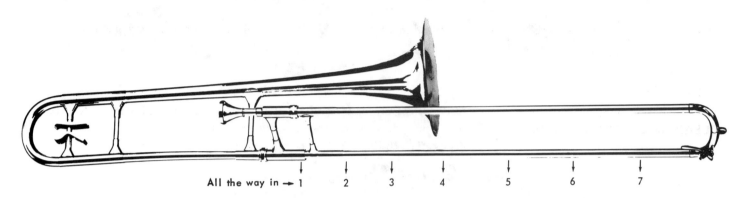

How To Read The Chart

The number of the position for each note is given in the chart below. See picture above for location of the slide and hand for each position. When two notes are given on the chart (F# and Gb), they are the same tone, and of course, played with the same position.

When two positions for a note are indicated, always use the TOP one unless your teacher tells you otherwise.

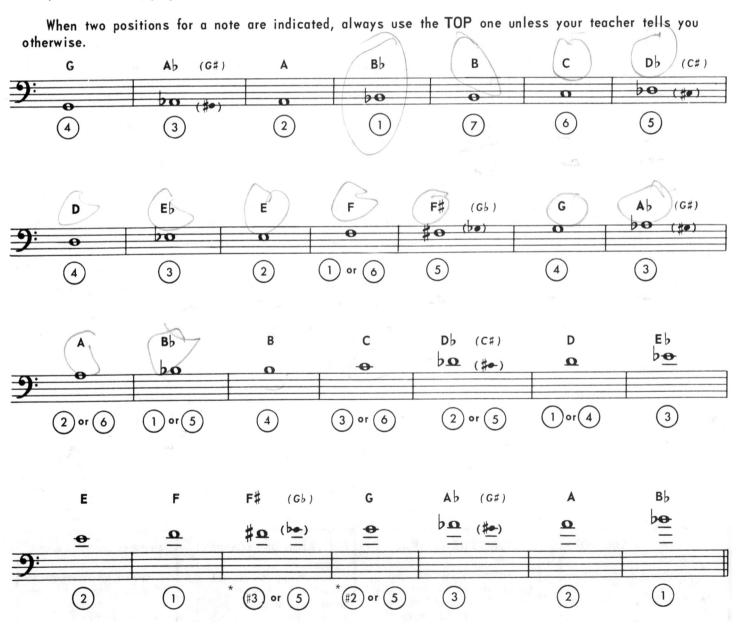

*The # is used to indicate a high position. (The slide should be in a little more than for the regular position.)

© 1969 (Renewed) BELWIN-MILLS PUBLISHING CORP.
All Rights Assigned to and Controlled by ALFRED PUBLISHING CO., INC.
All Rights Reserved

Getting Started

On the Trombone we can get several different tones with each slide position, by tightening or loosening the lips.

FIRST DO THIS —
Play any 1st position tone (slide all the way in). Hold it as long as COMFORTABLE and try to make it as CLEAR and STEADY as possible. Be sure the air goes through the horn in a steady stream.

The tone you play will probably be one of THREE tones. We will call them "HIGH", "MIDDLE", and "LOW". Your teacher will tell you which one you are playing.

_____ HIGH

_____ MIDDLE

_____ LOW

PRACTICE THE THREE NOTES ABOVE
Until you can play them with a steady and pleasant sound. Your teacher will tell you which note you are playing.

High tones are easier for some beginners while others find the low tones easier to play. Omit the High note or Low note if difficult.

NOW DO THIS — If the High notes are easier try the line below.

OR THIS — If the Low notes are easier to play, try this line.

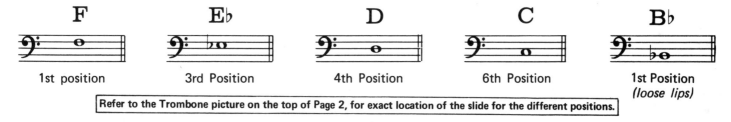

Refer to the Trombone picture on the top of Page 2, for exact location of the slide for the different positions.

If you can play both the HIGH and LOW notes, try playing the line below. Hold each tone as long as comfortable, and be sure each tone is clear and steady.

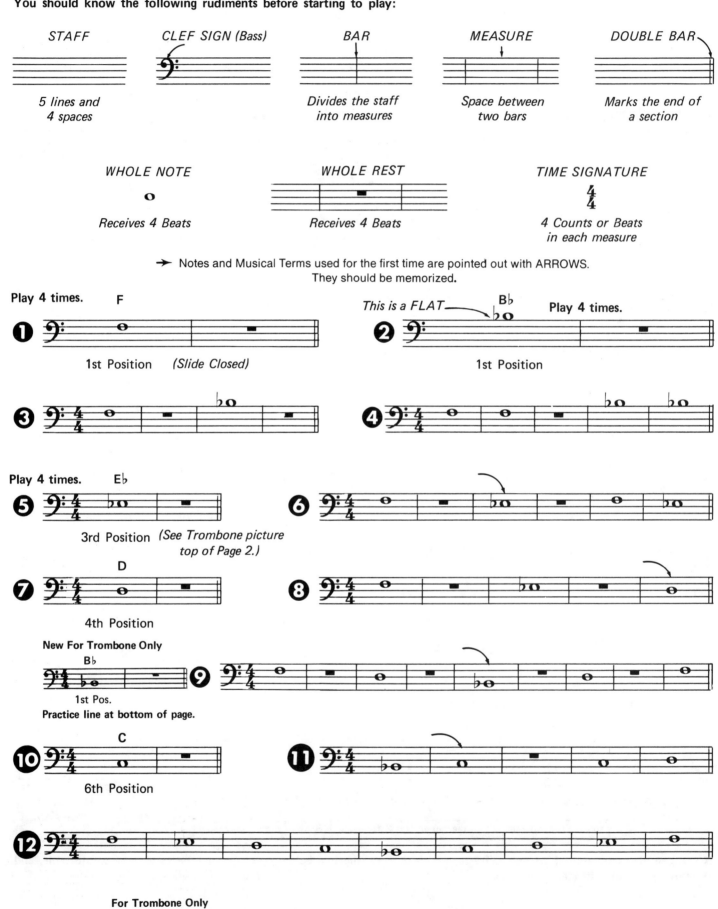

Lesson 2

Quarter Notes And Quarter Rests

Lesson 3

Special Page For Trombone Only

Up to this point we have "tongued" all notes. From here on, some will be tongued and others will be slurred. A "slur" is indicated by a curved line joining two or more notes. It looks like a "tie" but joins DIFFERENT notes. When two notes are slurred we tongue the first one but play the second either without tonguing or by tonguing softly with a "Doo".

Tonguing and slurring on the trombone is somewhat different than for other instruments because of the slide. The studies and suggestions on this page should help you understand the first principles of proper trombone tonguing and slurring. Practice this page carefully and follow your teacher's suggestions because proper tonguing is very important on the trombone.

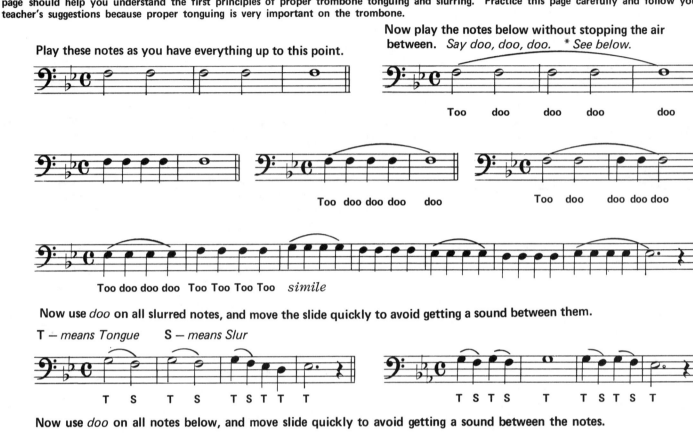

Now use *doo* on all slurred notes, and move the slide quickly to avoid getting a sound between them.

T — means Tongue   S — means Slur

Now use *doo* on all notes below, and move slide quickly to avoid getting a sound between the notes.

Use *doo* on all notes but move slide quickly and *keep the air flowing.*

ALTERNATE POSITIONS

Some notes on the trombone can be played in more than one position. These additional positions are called *"Alternate Positions"*. It is very important to learn HOW and WHEN to use these alternate positions because it leads to faster and smoother playing as you progress. They are absolutely essential in more advanced trombone playing. Additional information on alternate positions will be given where appropriate.

The Fs must sound the same.

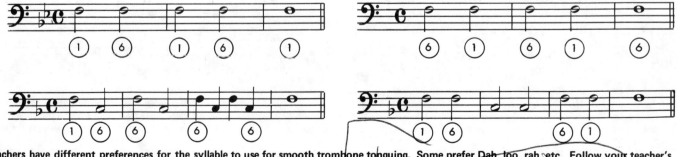

* Teachers have different preferences for the syllable to use for smooth trombone tonguing. Some prefer *Dah, Ioo, rah,* etc. Follow your teacher's preference.

B.I.C. 156

Our First Solo

On the top staff is a series of notes and rests. You are to rewrite this line on the bottom staff changing <u>notes</u> to <u>rests</u> of the same time value and <u>rests</u> to <u>notes</u> of the same time value.

Sample   etc.

Tongue one measure in regular manner, the next tongue using *doo*.

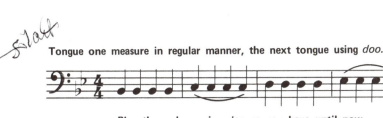

Play these slurs using *doo* as you have until now.

Now play the slurs with *NO* tongue except at the beginning of each slur.

Use *NO* tongue when slide stays in same position and you change notes. When you move the slide, tongue with *doo*.

Flat Keys

On the trombone we usually learn some of the *"Flat"* keys and scales first. This is because they are easier to play and the Young Band plays to a large extent in these keys (F, B♭, and A♭). You must be careful not to mix the "flats" and "naturals", especially E and A in the beginning.

The three lines below should help you distinguish clearly A, A♭, and A♮, and how they are affected by the Key Signature. Study them carefully.

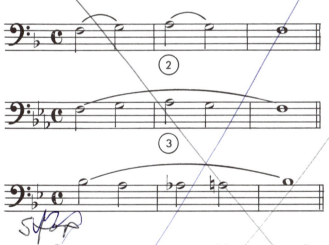
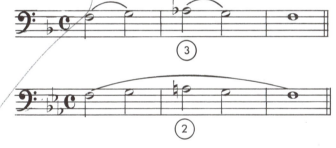

Alternate Position Studies

Some notes can be played in more than one position.
It is sometimes easier to use an alternate position because it doesn't require as much slide movement.

Most of the time F (4th line) is played 1st position but there are times, usually when going between F and 2nd space C, when there is an advantage in playing F in 6th position. The lines below will point this out.

In the line below, the student should decide which position is most logical.

Lesson 11

A Natural cancels a Flat (or sharp).

Church Song

This is written in the Key of B♭ to emphasize E♮ using a ♮ sign. See Number 5 for "Church Song" written in Key of F as it should be written.

There is only ONE Flat.
All E's are played E natural - (just plain E).

2 Flats

To remind you the note isn't E♭

Compare with No. 2. Notice how much easier it looks when written in Key of F and ♮ sign isn't necessary.
*See below.

Bicycle Built For Two

Double Note Duet

Student (or Teacher)

Teacher (or Student)

*When we have 1 Flat in the Key Signature, it is always B♭ and the Key is F. It means the piece is based on the scale of F. You must be careful to play E (2nd position) instead of E♭ (3rd position).

Lesson 13

Eighth Notes

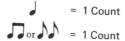

Play Number 1 first in 4/4 time - then in Cut (¢) Time. Then play Number 2 as written. Compare Number 1 played in ¢ time with Number 2 played in eighth notes.

Your teacher will show you his favorite way of counting eithth notes.

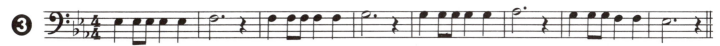

If the foot-tapping method of counting is used make sure the foot comes UP (Up beat) in EXACTLY the MIDDLE of the BEAT.

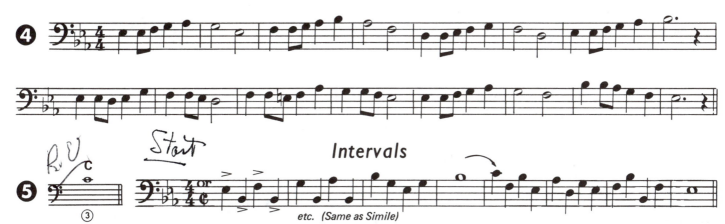

Intervals

etc. (Same as Simile)

Play slowly and separate tones. DO NOT STOP tone with the tongue.

Chromatics

Also play slurred.

Skip To M'Lou

Melody Fun

Play 3 times. The first time play the entire melody. 2nd time - omit all notes marked with ★ and substitute a rest.
3rd time - omit all notes marked ★ and + and substitute quarter rests.

1 Name the notes. **2** Mark fingering.

B.I.C. 156

Special Page For Trombone Only

Play these slurs with *doo* as you have until now.

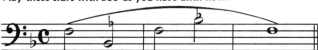 

Now play the slurs with NO tongue, except at the beginning of each slur.

On the 2 lines below, use *doo*, only when you move the slide; otherwise do not tongue except at the beginning of each slur.

The 3 lines below should help you distinguish clearly between E, E♭, and E♮ and how they are affected by the key signature. Study them carefully.

E♭ And E♮

High Notes

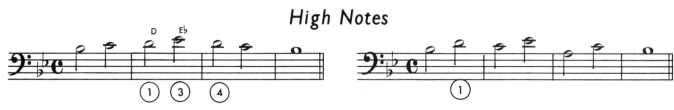

D is usually played 1st position but it can be played in the 4th position. It is usually played 4th position when between two 3rd position notes such as high C and E♭ or C and C or E♭ and E♭.

First play using your regular position for F, then play using positions as marked. Which is easier?

It may seem a little tricky to learn these alternate positions and when to use them, but when you have mastered their use your playing will become much easier and you will be able to play faster.

Lesson 16

Lesson 17

Lesson 18

Lesson 20

Lesson 21

A Page of Counting Fun
Carnival Of Venice
Theme And Nine Variations

TONGUING FUN - *Do not put tongue between the teeth.*

Lesson 23

Lesson 24

Lesson 25

Lesson 26

Lesson 27

Lesson 30

Lesson 32

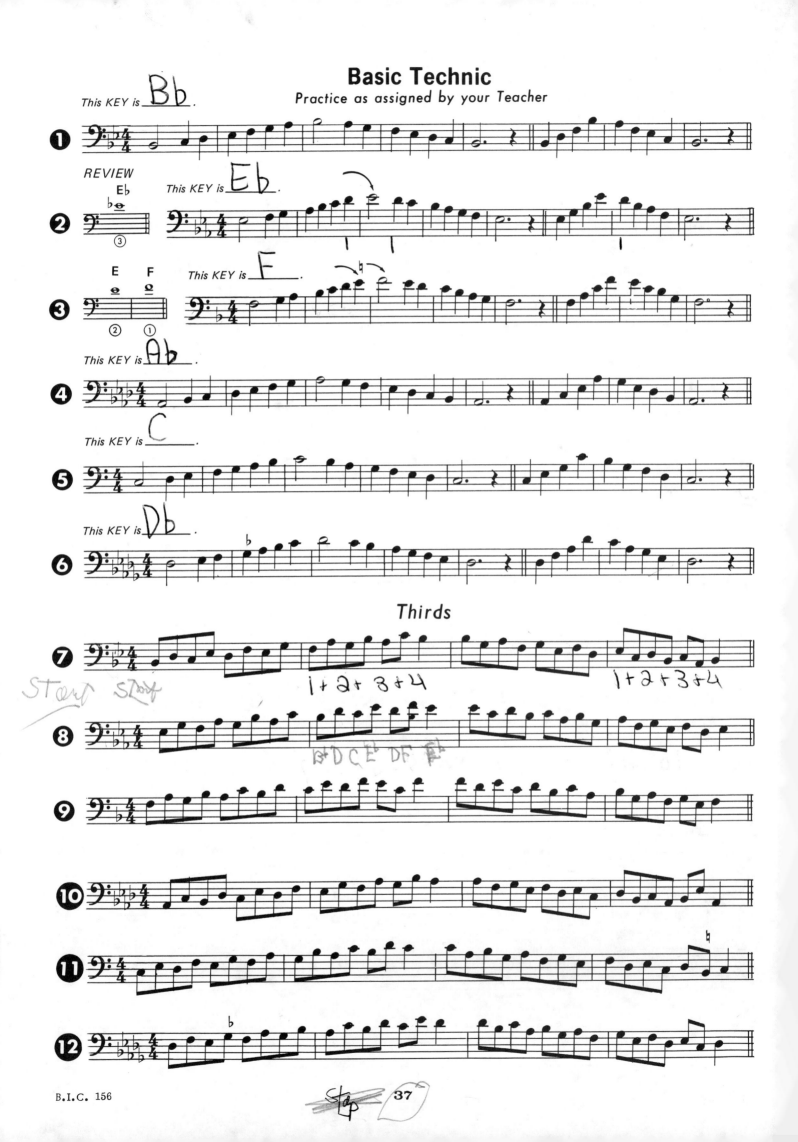

Range Builders
Special Page For Trombone Only

High Notes And Alternate D

D above the staff is usually played in 1st position but frequently it is best to play it in 4th position. It is usually played in 4th position when it comes between C and E♭; C and C; or E♭ and E♭. As a general rule, it is best to play it in the closest position or the position that requires the least slide movement.

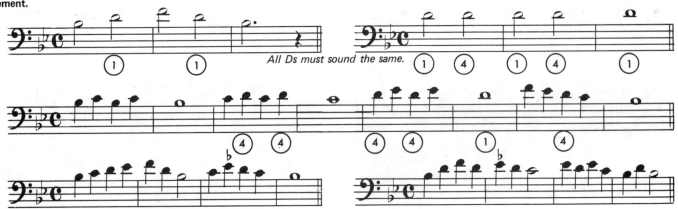

On the bottom line the student should decide which is the proper position for high D.

Basic Technic

The Patterns below provide for unlimited scale practice in the 7 most common band keys.

Start with ANY line and play through the entire pattern without stopping. Return to the STARTING LINE and play to where the END is marked. You must keep the KEY SIGNATURE of the STARTING LINE THROUGHOUT the entire pattern.

Chromatics

Speed Tests

Name the notes. Work for speed. Each test should be completed in 1 minute and 15 seconds or less.

Completed in ___ Seconds.

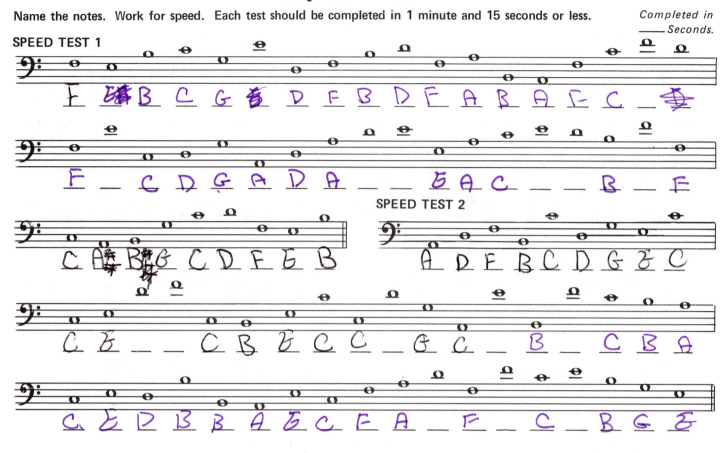

Home Practice Record

Week	Mon.	Tues.	Wed.	Thurs.	Fri.	Sat.	Sun. Total	Parent's Signature	Week	Mon.	Tues.	Wed.	Thurs.	Fri.	Sat.	Sun. Total	Parent's Signature
1	X	les.	60	0	0	30	150		21								
2	0	30	les.						22								
3	X		les.	0	0	60			23								
4									24								
5									25								
6									26								
7									27								
8									28								
9									29								
10									30								
11									31								
12									32								
13									33								
14									34								
15									35								
16									36								
17									37								
18									38								
19									39								
20									40								

PRACTICAL HINTS

Tips from the instrumental experts —
all in collaboration with James D. Ployhar

PRACTICAL HINTS is a unique and highly informative series developed to answer the many questions raised by the beginning student as well as the more advanced musician. Designed for individual use, the PRACTICAL HINTS books cover such vital topics as care and maintenance, reeds and mouthpieces, playing position, embouchure, tuning, tonguing, tone quality, range, and practice methodology. Each book has been written by a nationally known instrumental specialist in collaboration with James D. Ployhar. Serving as a handy and informative guide, an appropriate PRACTICAL HINTS book should be in every musician's library.

The PRACTICAL HINTS Series —

___ (EL 02700) **FLUTE** by Richard R. Hahn

___ (EL 02701) **Bb CLARINET** by Robert Lowry

___ (EL 02702) **ALTO CLARINET** by Arthur Nix

___ (EL 02703) **BASS CLARINET** by Arthur Nix

___ (EL 02704) **OBOE** by Earl Clemmens

___ (EL 02705) **BASSOON** by Roy D. Johnson

___ (EL 02706) **ALTO SAXOPHONE**
by Eugene Rousseau

___ (EL 02707) **TENOR SAXOPHONE**
by Eugene Rousseau

___ (EL 02708) **BARITONE SAXOPHONE**
by Eugene Rousseau

___ (EL 02709) **CORNET/TRUMPET**
by Robert E. Foster

___ (EL 02710) **FRENCH HORN** by David Bushouse

___ (EL 02711) **TROMBONE** by Paul Tanner

___ (EL 02712) **BARITONE** by Brian Bowman

___ (EL 02713) **TUBA** by Donald Little

___ (EL 02714) **PERCUSSION (Snare Drum,
Bass Drum, Timpani, Cymbals)**
by Wally Barnett

___ (EL 02715) **MALLET PERCUSSION**
by Wally Barnett

SOLO SOUNDS

Here, under one roof, is contained some of the most important solo material yet compiled — the SOLO SOUNDS Instrumental Series.

The contents of the SOLO SOUNDS folios feature works on **State Contest Lists** for each instrument (and pieces that are likely list candidates).

composers/arrangers include:

- William Bell
- Jaroslav Cimera
- Frank Erickson
- Dale Eyman
- Leonard Falcone
- Philip Farkas
- Ralph Guenther
- Bobby Herriot
- James Ployhar
- Eugene Rousseau
- Leonard Smith

Two folios are available for each instrument, both with supplementary piano accompaniment volumes.

All are organized for logical student advancement.

SOLO SOUNDS FOR FLUTE - Volume 1
___ (EL 03323) Levels 1 - 3 Solo Book
___ (EL 03324) Levels 1 - 3 Piano Acc.
___ (EL 03325) Levels 3 - 5 Solo Book
___ (EL 03326) Levels 3 - 5 Piano Acc.

SOLO SOUNDS FOR CLARINET - Volume 1
___ (EL 03331) Levels 1 - 3 Solo Book
___ (EL 03332) Levels 1 - 3 Piano Acc.
___ (EL 03333) Levels 3 - 5 Solo Book
___ (EL 03334) Levels 3 - 5 Piano Acc.

SOLO SOUNDS FOR OBOE - Volume 1
___ (EL 03327) Levels 1 - 3 Solo Book
___ (EL 03328) Levels 1 - 3 Piano Acc.
___ (EL 03329) Levels 3 - 5 Solo Book
___ (EL 03330) Levels 3 - 5 Piano Acc.

SOLO SOUNDS FOR ALTO SAXOPHONE - Volume 1
___ (EL 03335) Levels 1 - 3 Solo Book
___ (EL 03336) Levels 1 - 3 Piano Acc.
___ (EL 03337) Levels 3 - 5 Solo Book
___ (EL 03338) Levels 3 - 5 Piano Acc.

SOLO SOUNDS FOR TRUMPET - Volume 1
___ (EL 03339) Levels 1 - 3 Solo Book
___ (EL 03340) Levels 1 - 3 Piano Acc.
___ (EL 03341) Levels 3 - 5 Solo Book
___ (EL 03342) Levels 3 - 5 Piano Acc.

SOLO SOUNDS FOR TROMBONE - Volume 1
___ (EL 03347) Levels 1 - 3 Solo Book
___ (EL 03348) Levels 1 - 3 Piano Acc.
___ (EL 03349) Levels 3 - 5 Solo Book
___ (EL 03350) Levels 3 - 5 Piano Acc.

SOLO SOUNDS FOR FRENCH HORN - Volume 1
___ (EL 03343) Levels 1 - 3 Solo Book
___ (EL 03344) Levels 1 - 3 Piano Acc.
___ (EL 03345) Levels 3 - 5 Solo Book
___ (EL 03346) Levels 3 - 5 Piano Acc.

SOLO SOUNDS FOR TUBA - Volume 1
___ (EL 03351) Levels 1 - 3 Solo Book
___ (EL 03352) Levels 1 - 3 Piano Acc.
___ (EL 03353) Levels 3 - 5 Solo Book
___ (EL 03354) Levels 3 - 5 Piano Acc.

A superior series at a most reasonable price.

From the Baroque to the 20th Century
CLASSICAL INSTRUMENTAL ENSEMBLES FOR ALL
CLASSICAL DUETS FOR ALL • CLASSICAL TRIOS FOR ALL
CLASSICAL QUARTETS FOR ALL
Arranged by William Ryden

Any combination and any number of instruments can play together in harmony. Woodwinds, brass, strings and percussion can have fun playing in like instrument or mixed instrument ensembles.

These collections of keyboard, vocal and instrumental pieces cover a wide range of styles and music by composers from the Baroque to the 20th Century periods.

All the music is carefully graded from Level I to Level IV. Alternate musical passages and octaves are provided for some of the selections to allow the player more choices when needed.

The pages are laid out in an identical manner in each book so that all performers can quickly locate a point for discussion or rehearsal. No page turns are required when playing.

This set of books will meet the needs of classmates, friends, family and neighbors who want to play together in school, in church or at the mall. This is also an outstanding tool for auditions, sight reading and learning the art of ensemble playing. These are all-purpose folios that make classical music fun!

CLASSICAL DUETS FOR ALL • CLASSICAL TRIOS FOR ALL • CLASSICAL QUARTETS FOR ALL
fit your every need!

CLASSICAL DUETS FOR ALL
(17 titles)
(EL96127) Piano/Conductor, Oboe
(EL96128) Flute, Piccolo
(EL96129) B♭ Clarinet, Bass Clarinet
(EL96130) Alto Saxophone
　(E♭ Saxes and E♭ Clarinets)
(EL96131) Tenor Saxophone
(EL96132) B♭ Trumpet, Baritone T.C.
(EL96133) Horn in F
(EL96134) Trombone, Baritone B.C.,
　Bassoon, Tuba
(EL96135) Violin
(EL96136) Viola
(EL96137) Cello/Bass
(EL96138) Percussion

CLASSICAL TRIOS FOR ALL
(15 titles)
(EL96139) Piano/Conductor, Oboe
(EL96140) Flute, Piccolo
(EL96141) B♭ Clarinet, Bass Clarinet
(EL96142) Alto Saxophone
　(E♭ Saxes and E♭ Clarinets)
(EL96143) Tenor Saxophone
(EL96144) B♭ Trumpet, Baritone T.C.
(EL96145) Horn in F
(EL96146) Trombone, Baritone B.C.,
　Bassoon, Tuba
(EL96147) Violin
(EL96148) Viola
(EL96149) Cello/Bass
(EL96150) Percussion

CLASSICAL QUARTETS FOR ALL
(13 titles)
(EL96151) Piano/Conductor, Oboe
(EL96152) Flute, Piccolo
(EL96153) B♭ Clarinet, Bass Clarinet
(EL96154) Alto Saxophone
　(E♭ Saxes and E♭ Clarinets)
(EL96155) Tenor Saxophone
(EL96156) B♭ Trumpet, Baritone T.C.
(EL96157) Horn in F
(EL96158) Trombone, Baritone B.C.,
　Bassoon, Tuba
(EL96159) Violin
(EL96160) Viola
(EL96161) Cello/Bass
(EL96162) Percussion

INSTRUMENTAL ENSEMBLES FOR ALL
DUETS FOR ALL • TRIOS FOR ALL • QUARTETS FOR ALL
by Albert Stoutamire and Kenneth Henderson

Any combination and any number of instruments can play together in harmony. Woodwinds, brass, strings, and mallet percussion (even snare drum in **DUETS FOR ALL**) can have fun playing in like instrument or mixed instrument ensembles.

The material covers a wide range of styles and music by composers from Baroque through contemporary eras.

DUETS FOR ALL and **TRIOS FOR ALL** range in difficulty from grades I through IV. **QUARTETS FOR ALL** range in difficulty from grades I through III.

The pages are laid out in an identical manner in each book so that performers can quickly locate a point for discussion or rehearsal. No page turning is required while playing.

This set of books meets the needs of classmates, friends, family and neighbors who wish to play together for festivals, concerts or just for fun. They are also excellent for learning ensemble playing, auditions and sight reading.

DUETS FOR ALL • TRIOS FOR ALL • QUARTETS FOR ALL fit your every need!

 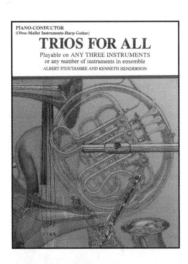 

DUETS FOR ALL
Stoutamire and Henderson

(PROBK 01337) **Piano Conductor, Mallets**
(PROBK 01324) **Flute, Piccolo**
(PROBK 01325) **Oboe, Guitar**
(PROBK 01326) **Bb Clarinet, Bass Clarinet**
(PROBK 01327) **Eb Saxes, Eb Clarinets**
(PROBK 01328) **Tenor Saxophone**
(PROBK 01329) **Cornet, Baritone T.C.**
(PROBK 01330) **F Horn**
(PROBK 01331) **Trombone, Baritone, Bassoon**
(PROBK 01332) **Tuba**
(PROBK 01333) **Snare Drum**
(PROBK 01334) **Violin**
(PROBK 01335) **Viola**
(PROBK 01336) **Cello & Bass**

TRIOS FOR ALL
Stoutamire and Henderson

(PROBK 01402) **Piano, Conductor, Oboe, Mallets**
(PROBK 01392) **Flute, Piccolo**
(PROBK 01393) **Bb Clarinet, Bass Clarinet**
(PROBK 01394) **Cornet**
(PROBK 01395) **Eb Saxes, Eb Clarinets**
(PROBK 01396) **F Horn**
(PROBK 01397) **Trombone, Baritone B.C., Bassoon, Tuba**
(PROBK 01398) **Baritone T.C.**
(PROBK 01399) **Violin**
(PROBK 01400) **Viola**
(PROBK 01401) **Cello, Bass**

QUARTETS FOR ALL
Stoutamire and Henderson

(PROBK 01435) **Piano Conductor, Mallets**
(PROBK 01427) **C Treble Instruments**
(PROBK 01428) **Bb Treble Instruments**
(PROBK 01429) **Eb Treble Instruments**
(PROBK 01430) **F Instruments**
(PROBK 01431) **Bass Clef Instruments**
(PROBK 01432) **Violin**
(PROBK 01433) **Viola**
(PROBK 01434) **Cello, Bass**

This music is available at your local music dealer.